Smallholding

Also by Anne Compton

Poetry

Alongside
Asking Questions Indoors and Out
Processional
Opening the Island

Prose

Afterwork: Essays on Literature and Beauty
Meetings with Maritime Poets
A. J. M. Smith: Canadian Metaphysical

Editor

The Edge of Home: Milton Acorn from the Island (editor)
Coastlines: The Poetry of Atlantic Canada (co-editor)

Smallholding

Anne Compton

Fitzhenry & Whiteside

Published in Canada by Fitzhenry & Whiteside,
195 Allstate Parkway, Markham, ON L3R 4T8

Published in the United States by Fitzhenry & Whiteside,
311 Washington Street, Brighton, MA 02135

Fitzhenry & Whiteside acknowledges with thanks the Canada Council for the Arts and the Ontario Arts Council for their support of our publishing program.

ONTARIO ARTS COUNCIL
CONSEIL DES ARTS DE L'ONTARIO
an Ontario government agency
un organisme du gouvernement de l'Ontario

Canada Council for the Arts
Conseil des arts du Canada

Library and Archives Canada Cataloguing in Publication
FeldTitle: Smallholding / by Anne Compton.
Names: Compton, Anne, author.
Description: Poems.
Identifiers: Canadiana 20190053585 | ISBN 9781554554683 (softcover)
Classification: LCC PS8555.O5185 S63 2019 | DDC C811/.6—dc23

Publisher Cataloging-in-Publication Data (U.S.)
Title: Smallholding / Anne Compton.
Description: Markham, Ontario : Fitzhenry & Whiteside, 2019. | Includes bibliography. | Summary: "Poetry that turns to everyday things and occasions, recalling the persons, places and objects which form the constituents of life" – Provided by publisher.
Identifiers: ISBN 978-1-55455-468-3 (paperback)
Subjects: LCSH: Canadian poetry – 21st century. | BISAC: POETRY / General.
Classification: LCC PN9195.72C667 | DDC 811.6 – dc23

10 9 8 7 6 5 4 3 2 1

Cover painting *Storm Doors*, oil/tempera on panel, by Richard Davis. His work can be found at rtdavis.com
Text and cover design by Karen Thomas
Printed in Canada by Copywell

www.fitzhenry.ca

for John William Smith, i.m.

and for

Aaron and Quentin, Theresa and Robbie

Contents

Provisions

Onion 11
Supper, The Iliad 12
Tablecloth and Other Compound Words 13
Wifecakes 14
The Pair of Us 15
Not himself 16
The Supper-painter considers *The Symposium* 17
Patterns, Palm Sunday 18
Heaven 19

Sleep

Storm Windows 23
Sleeping in the Spare 24
The River in Spring 25
Waterways 26
Mowed Field 27
Fishing Boats, December Morning 28
Dream as Misnomer 29
Morning, convex mirror 30
Sleep Knots 31
Asleep on the Coast 32
Revelation, March 1st 33

Travel

Rest Stop 37
Some night 38
Reading Montaigne 39
De Kooning's Door 40
Wild Honeysuckle 41

Son 42
Zero 43
Truth and Invention 44
Dear _________, 45
Onrush 46
The Extra 47
Three Waltzes That Haven't Names 48
Vernal Wedding 50
Rain, Versailles 51
With Tomas and Bertie at the Sallyforth Café 52
Lear Prunes the Black Currant Bush 53
Sex and Death at the Natural History Museum 54

The Mind at sixes and sevens

The Brain is – Wider than the Sky – 59
How Memory Works 60
Unfinished 61
Trees, Yuletide 62
Sun After 63
The rarity of white birds 64
The Shotgun in Gainsborough's Landscape 65
Talk Puts an End to Time 66
In the small hours 67
Swimmers 68
Window 69
Evening, a resistance 70
Root 71
Letter 72
Tree 73

Notes 75
Acknowledgements 76

Provisions

Who despises the day of small things?
Zechariah 4:10

Onion

Weighs more than it looks: *Should do*, my father says, bent among
October rows. I've come the yellow corridors to be with him.

Like a star compacted by gravity – that dense.
Nebula of particles, fused and lit. *Unus*, its Latin name.

Best dug at first frost: Difficult, though, to be rid of the soil specks
in the outer sheath. Iron flavour in the winter sandwich.

Graded by flesh colour and as to keeping – storage or straight away.

The Vidalia, in pale-coloured skin, similar to all things fresh –
sweetest forthwith. Thick-skinned storage, a deeper flavour.

Decades gone, he's likely starlight. Or he's the data
encrypted in cells. My cells. The inside story's never lost.

Heaven from earth, according to him. Readable parchment –
in layers – had we the cipher to decode it. Circle by circle.

At the root-end, there are tear-producing compounds,
where it gripped earth. This is true of all things temporary.

About this part, turn aside at the last.

Supper, *The Iliad*

Achilles cooked for Priam in the Achaean camp.

Priam who had come a life's distance for the body
of his battle-slain son. Burial clothes in the cart.

Also in there the ransom red cloaks.

Crossing the flatland in the dark and the quiet.

The grief-spent frugality of mule and wagon.

The walls of Achilles' tent surged and settled in the requiem wind.

Two of them now – *the sound of mourning moving in the house.*

With his own hands, Achilles slaughtered the lamb, roasted and served it.
The old man and the young. The feeling between them – except that.

After the bread and the wine and the meat, Priam slept in the porch.
Sheltered from the Achaeans by *man-slaughtering* Achilles.

As soon as dawn yellowed the flatland, the Trojan king set out for Ilion,
the weight of the beautified body with him in the mule-drawn cart.

Tablecloth and Other Compound Words

At the seamed horizon, there is – of all things – a damask,
patterned on both sides, reversible. The near side's
a flapping reflection, somewhat faded, of what's below.

The wind-ruffled edge of the reverse uncurls a similar scene
though the nap's unworn: Threads bright from the loom.
How it was, or will be.

2

The tablecloth, starch-stiff, on the linen rack. Napkins
stacked on a *sideboard*: A word plain as *windowpane*.
Those doubles, whose job it is to reveal. The compound's
recursive: One thing inside another.

In the diningroom, smelling of wood and beeswax,
the everyday's exaggerated by a spareleaf.
When the alb-white's unfolded – atop the underskirt –
it curves to the oval. Takes shape. Followed by plate,
cutlery, stemware – wine, water, wine – aligned to a knife.
A received geometry. Step away with me. See it
through the French doors. A cabinet of modest hope.

3

On the way to the kitchen, I check the dictionary:
syde-borde, in use for seven centuries. Halfway
between then and now, Anonymous made a note:
It has more the air of an altar than the table has.

Same century as the Dutch paintings where women work
with their backs to us, bent to a basket – medlars, perhaps –
peelings falling from their laps. A radiant scutwork:

You get the gods you work for. Theirs, and mine, a skygod
who knows ceremony's for an hour, not a lifetime.

Wifecakes

On the last day of December every family's obliged
to use up any flour left in the house. Durum and spelt.

This is called eating the old year.

The wives make battercakes, milky thin,
set the table with dinner plates.

All who are old enough for the table name the year's troubles,
fold a wifecake 'round their words.

Things you say in the mind, not aloud.

Passing your plate to the right, taking the one
on your left, you nod in gratitude.

It doesn't hurt to eat another's pain,
and it's a help to them. In some families,

the affliction cakes are fed to the pigs
or buried in the garden if ground can be dug.

Wearing fresh clothes, you stand on the doorstep.
Welcome without words the year you're ready
to begin. Sip tea without milk.

The Pair of Us

What is the taste of rain, we wondered. Took our bread outside, held the slices aloft.
Raindrops pearled on the butter. *Pluvial perfection*, you said. *Sky broth*.

Another time – this was winter – we hid the Christmas oranges in the woodshed,
waited for the right kind of snow. Compactable. Crows hauled at the peelings
while we ate orange snowballs.
                                        Eaters of elements, we taste-tested the imaginable.
Chefs, you said, *have to be full of themselves*.

In springtime, we rarely showed up for meals, preferred a midnight supper
while the house slept. Cooked coddled eggs in pondwater: A lard tin
suspended over a firepit in the woods.

Foraged, though not for the foods – dandelion greens, stinging nettle –
Gran talked about. Towards morning, we kneaded pilfered bread into pellets,
trailed them house to woods.
                                        When you held your arms out, grackles lit
on your wrists. Soon as they settled, you opened your fists, offered oat flakes
soaked in tree sap. All of us sipped and ate. The grackles' bronze feathers,
in among the dark, shone with a light centuries old.

Two years younger, I was sous-chef to your best notion: What's indoors
must be brought out, changed back. A Paleolithic version of pantry.

Before I was, you *were*, but not quite. Born unfinished, your bones hadn't hardened.
Spent your crib days with a calcium drip in your arm while your skeleton took shape.
A caudal remnant at the tip of your spine.

We took our first steps together. Our twinned minds correcting
a mismanaged calendar.

Not himself

Set a place for the stranger, my father would say every supper. And we would. Only to take it away, untouched, at the end of the meal. We often had guests, though none that were strangers, unless of course one of the guests was the stranger in disguise. *Set a place for the stranger*, and all us kids would answer, *The second stranger*, not that we knew why there should be a second when there hadn't been a first, but it's what he wanted. One time, after the meal, when one of the older ones, carrying the lamp, was taking her up the stairs to bed, Cassie asked, *Who is the first already come*? Cassie was like that, bolder in her words.

Of course it didn't happen every day of my childhood. It just seems that way. Something must have happened to my father to make him say that for the first time, and then carry on with it as if it were a charm or spell. This was in the days when people were put in the sanatorium – the San – for the influenza cure, but the San was also the asylum, and there was a period when my father was in there for his nerves, that is, until he escaped and made his way home. That was in spring and all through the summer he worked in the vegetable garden, enlarging it three times its size. He'd always been a great one for putting-by.

Soon enough he seemed back to himself, or what, to me, looked familiar. When the twins were born, he said it was proof, but what it proved, I couldn't figure out. Then one evening at supper he laid down his spoon and uttered again the benediction or whatever it was. A look of horror passed over my mother's face and the child in her lap whimpered, buried its face in my mother's collar. But this time it was more whisper than command, and he took up his soupspoon straight away. No, that's not right. He said it cheerfully, as if in thanks: *The stranger in his place.*

The Supper-painter considers *The Symposium*

But what concerns us at present is that Diotima was my instructress in the art of love.
Socrates

After the meal, when it's time to talk, the flute-girl's sent off.

No need for chairs. The table's low to the ground. But what of the cloth
and the dishes? Through which window does the light fall, gilding
the bronzes? These are the things a woman needs to know: But where
in this room am I? From what angle might I sort my surroundings,
render the supper things, yet withstand the defamation I'm hearing?

The reclining men, turn-taking, revolve their thoughts:
In the absence of women they speak of love, praise it,
but not for the woman's part. Her beauty is the baser sort.

This kind, Heavenly Love, being motherless, is without stain
or so Pausanias says, and none of the well-fed disagree:
Common love cannot make a man *go aright*.

Socrates, shod (unusual for him), and waylaid by a thought (usual for him),
arrives late to the meal. Doesn't matter. The meal's the talk. And talk's the thing.

Except for him, they are young and shining, and what anyway
would a person say about beauty if he were satyr-ugly? (Savonarola,
in another age, broke or burned whatever could cause a stumble –
all the beautiful bodies words go in fear of.)

The listeners, in lounging attitude, frame the satyr's say-so.
Flushed faces tilted upward to follow his aerial perspective:
Socrates' words stepping aloft and away. Wrought-iron
is how I see the staircase taking shape in the fumy air.

A woman's sent out at the start, a woman's let in at the last:
A device is what the scholars call her. She'd have to be, wouldn't she?

But what I love is the beauty of her feet on the stairway.

Patterns, Palm Sunday

Our epiphanies inseparable from our chores.
Jonah Lehrer

We're tethered to objects. Or beholden to them. Patterns of wear in the kitchen's bare-board floor.
Not like that hypocritical room, sometimes called *living*, where we don't. No one does.
It's here – stove to sink; sink to shelf – that a chipped cup can become a chalice.

For the painter, the women *come into existence with the rooms we see them in.*

2

A drop-leaf table, scrubbed clean. At its centre a bread-and-butter plate, turquoise with gold rim.
Three green figs, the globe of them so translucent the jellied pulp shines through.
Two of them leant together, the third toppled over, the tip of its stem touching the rim.

The sink-window shows me a red cardinal motionless on the snowcrust.
When I go out to him, he turns his seed-black eye on me. But doesn't move.
There, there. Stroke his head and his wings. He's much smaller than I'd expected.

Had seen him last summer – this cardinal or another – at the birdfeeder.
The seeds he'd picked up there, he carried below
to the fledglings – a feathery green pair – mouth-open, on the verandah railing.

This is the day that used to be called Fig Sunday, one week before Easter.
There are fidgets of snow in the spring air – a flock of utterances.

When I follow the fluttering bird into the colonnade of trees,
spruce and pine predicate an earthy eternity.

Heaven

Sure there'll be a meal there – we're promised that – or at least an arrival-repast,
one that'll appease a hunger we've had a long time, not that we'll be checking
our watches or looking at clocks, and, of course, there'll be no night nor day.
At that first meal, the newcomers – shifting in their chairs, scanning the crowd –
– will take no notice of him, the Lord at the end of the table, not the head of it,
laughing softly at all the chatter, the chaos – someone kicking a briefcase
under the table, another sifting his pockets for a pack of smokes – a settling in
that could go on forever.

Sleep

Storm Windows

Things needed in fall: Crops brought in, the house banked, storms over screens, more sleep. By September, the children slept longer. The grown-ups, with so much to do, held off, but when the first frosts crisped the grass, they too were sleeping ten to twelve hours.

When the heavy snows started, waking was less than sleeping; the daylit hours, an interval.

Jobs got done: Cattle milked and fed, horses exercised; the stable, in afternoon, bedded with fresh straw, the last so carefully done as if they, like us, were entering upon a nightwork that required mattressing.

The days, I'd say, were touched by tenderness, a separateness existing between us as if each person were a stranger stopping by, deserving the utmost civility. Some days, the older sisters did lessons in the parlour with the younger. Letters and numbers, when they said them, were shapes held up to a window, chapped hands examining the sound, front and back.

Everything said – and it wasn't much – was like that, had heft. The habit of daytime talk was lost, each word a hand-weight. A house of sleepers, yes, but as my grandmother warned, Sleep, you can see. The dream, you can't.

If you think I'm relating us to the dormant – the dormice in their bed of leaves, bats vertical in caves – you'd be wrong. Vigilant dreaming, at the heart of winter sleep, retaliates the dark. As necessary to survival as the several uses of tallow.

Sleeping in the Spare

It's the dusk, not the night, causes the lurch. After that,
you're saddling a horse in the dark. The huff of its breath, ashen.

When leaving, face into the wind. Have it at your back
returning. Carry conviction.

In the secular night, you enter others' dreams, belong to no one.
Whether in the body or apart from the body, I do not know. God knows.

Who gets up in the morning is not who went to bed.
A sleeper turning over, not waking, is doing shift work.

You see one of the sisters in the hallway. Then, the mind adjusts.
This is what mirrors are for: Catching the self side-on.

A magic trick depends on misdirection: Concentrate on the frame.
In the fraction you're away, anything might slip in.

Hearing's the fastest sense, but the dark's a deafening silence.
Hold fast to the mane, the breathing slow and raspy.

In the winter bed where the widow sleeps, the horse
ran away with a cartload of memory. Be warned.

If there's a flitch of dawn, turn your face to it.
Head for the stair room, the hallway belongs to the sisters.

The upstairs window looks North; the downstairs –
same wall – faces South.

The dark, in the day, in the house is the eleventh effect.

The River in Spring

Over night the ice went out, or so we thought.
But it hadn't. An entire continent of it loosened
at the edges and went under. Whole cloth, as they say.

Had we been at the brink, we'd have seen the water chimney
collapse shoreward. Opposite shore, the same.

Some few heard it in their sleep, dreamed Niagara.
Woke to fish-littered trees and a water surface eerily
composed, the way a child colours a body of water stiff
with brightest blue.

Wakened, though, would be the wrong word.

The glaciated riverbed – ice sheet intact – drew down
the sunlight, reflected it back in columnar extravagance

while here on the shore some version of dawn wasn't leaving –

hasn't for days, its grey pressed close to the cloistered
light, the acoustic of the two things rubbing together,
Adagio di molto, Sibelius-sad.

A spurious story, the medic will say. His therapeutic voice
explaining how spring sickness – an affliction of sleepiness –
can overtake the mind while body adjusts to season.
Whole villages, he claims, are asleep in themselves, nightwalking.

Meanwhile, the children, fly-fishing the trees,
pile brook-bright trophies on soggy shore.

Waterways

For ten, eleven hours, she said, we go away from the body, which
Don't worry, has its woolly blankets, hot water bottles, rum tonic.
The little animal doesn't need much.

The night cabbie, sculling here and there,
ferries the brief, disconnected dreams of sleepers through city streets.
Still, if you know how to do it, the itinerary can be continuous,
a fluent disclosure, one night to the next. A network of canals,
each one intimate with doorways.

There'd be bridges to manoeuvre, wouldn't there, a suspension
over a timeworn estuary it's best to avoid.

Chancy, I know, but the alternative's an illiteracy of sorts.

Look at you, a third of your life you know nothing about.
Morning's yellow smear is a barge-lamp for looking back.
While you live, the sleeper can be roused, made to tell.

A certain state of mind knows. There are step-words for this.

Mowed Field

In daylight we see the edges of it over the river,
its tattered bit of drapery in the trees.
At night, though, the mist and the dark merge,
a pitchy dampness mantling the face.

Sleepless women, miles apart, meet in the fingering
dark. Not that they leave their beds.
Restlessness – wearing a shapeless shift – vacates the room,
steps edgeways into the blur. Latched windows, no obstacle.

Night is the opposite of fact, and mist its multiplier.

They could be sisters or cousins. Or, lovers.
Whichever, the piece of night, inside each, has sought the other.

One comes downslope, the other up, meeting in the mowed field.
The twist of river gives off an enamelling light.

When we were boys, one of them says, we were here.
When we led the horses to water, there were grackles –
portions of blueblack night in the daytime trees, and before that,
when we weren't anything, I knew you by the dark's thrum.

Lives aback this life is the story drifting over the shorn field
even though their houses are full of sleeping children.

Fishing Boats, December Morning

Often as they've heard the sermon of the sure foundation,
they know water guttering a hillside needs a way through.
There's not a cellar here that hasn't a runnel.
It's nothing to wake to its rustle a storey or two below.

They've learned to live with its indoor insinuations.

Deep frost weeks before, and rain over days.
Done now, but for the pooling. Nowhere to go.
The hallucinatory grass feigns uprightness
while mossed tree-bark verifies glitter-green.
Even gravel's lit. Asphalt too, and roofs, O red
of the tanager's wing. How sheen happens.

Out in the harbour five men in a boat – their traps
hauled up – head for shore. The brightening distance,
a beacon. Sometimes though, what gutters in the night
gets into sleep, breathes the black fear lapping gunnels.

Dream as Misnomer

They go out from us but they are not really of us.
This, after they've given us sleep and in that sleep
stories to deflect us from their absence. Dispatches
from the past, we mistake for *dreams*: Our word, not theirs.
Quickened by the dark, they are what wakes when we sleep.
Savants of uncivilized night. Nightwalkers. Senior to us –
as theropods are to songbirds – they know night's wed
to time by the whorls and folds of its ancient escarpment.

In morning's after-rain quiet, when birds recall flight,
you might hear someone below starting up the day.
Nailing the domestic to daybreak: Rearranging mud and twigs.
By then, the stranger – who is not you and yet yours –
is slouching in the brainstem. Welcome back the stranger.

Morning, convex mirror

Every morning there's the settling in, as if we'd moved house overnight.

Habit, an elderly housemate, fills the kettle at a tap,
finds the missing cardigan slung on a chair back.

Children's bodies, they say, lengthen while they sleep, gain definition –
unlike the aging nighttime mind which refuses any. Every day
less comfortable in the outsized body.

In the indeterminate hour, we're several.

The way grandmama addressed me in the third-person: *Sure, hasn't she
slept long? And would she like beet greens for breakfast, that bit of sausage
from last night's supper?* Assumed everyone was multiple.

The rippled looking glass in the hallway, no help at all.

If I were more distinct, I might see her still – out there in the garden –
pinching off greens. A plaid headscarf and blue gansey against the damp.
The height of her past the corn rows. Her bent, mine to come.

In the *Arnolfini Portrait*, he looks at them, they look at him,
all agreeing *Johannes de Eyck was here*.

That might be possible in a painting, but here it's harder.

Sleep Knots

I hated the morning's half-hour when grandmama worked the sleep knots from my hair before braiding it. Cross-over braids that had to be pinned in place. Beneath those razory fingers, her words probed the meaning of my dreams. Other times, she spoke of what dreaming does. *The day's direction*, she'd say, *is given us at night. Sleep does memory-work, sorts the new in relation to the old, makes tomorrow possible.*

The half-dozen hairpins I held in readiness, damp in my palm. Her voice above and behind me: *Some say, dream's the most of repose. Don't believe it. That kind of sorting causes a racket.* I'd nod my crown of braids in agreement.

The old men, past fieldwork, were with us there in the wood-stove kitchen. Pouring his tea into a saucer, a mouthful at a time, Uncle Ollie would sometimes say between sips, *Slept the wrong way.* As if it were a matter of travel and there'd been a wrong turning, but whether the error was his or mine, I never knew. *There can be no false turnings in the dark*, the even-older Septimus claimed. *While the horse is ridden, the heart's awake in the sleeper, pursuing a direction you know nothing of.*

Every day the same talk, the same gospel eyes holding me fast.

They were ancient and fair those convenors of my childhood, and what I know now – now that I am of their age – is this, It's about who's in the room.

Asleep on the Coast

August happened over night: *Been and gone*, the sound of the seawash.
It's packed the ripening days away, lowered them into the sea's cooler temperature.
Preserved, but not so as we can see them separately.

The guard stationed at Waking stops up our night knowledge. In there,
yesterday, and all the days before, desponded.

We're chastened by what we've let vanish: The blowsy hydrangea toppling
over a rail fence, colluding with the blackberry, those runaways.

Still, the birds, early morning, are worth waking up for.

And the trees – those stalwart citizens – emerging from fog,
their interlaced crowns looking, for all the world, like
tulip merchants bent to their sums in a Dutch painting,
the foresight of blooms in the massing of figures.

Revelation, March 1st

Because frost has lifted the larkspur clear of ground
I muck decayed manure around bared roots. Tamp gently.
An aroma of thaw and compost. Blend of what's past
what's to come – an incense of sorts. Didn't the apostle say
prayer's an aroma rising. Mine here, in the New Jerusalem.

John of Patmos, how'll we see roots uttering
seasonal news beneath streets of translucent gold?
And those gates of pearl, what'll they keep away?
I'm worried, John, about sleep where there's no night,
and if there's no sleep, how can there be stories?

Travel

Rest Stop

I was in the mirror
when she tapped me on the shoulder, called me Mary.
The face in the mirror couldn't be certain.

We went into the café for a coffee, and she asked after
my-Mary husband. Hadn't the heart to tell her
I wasn't, and hadn't. Not a husband to speak of.

Not so odd we'd meet here. Like truckers,
we had the habit of a fixed stop.

Later, I put my car on the weigh-scale: No tonnage.
Fiddled the radio dial stuck between stations.

Further on, and another province, a cliff sign warned
flying stones. Could be marl migrating for winter
or the dead ascending, mineral deposits
falling from wingtips.

The ancients say, a traveller should carry two tunics.
They haven't a word to say about the double life.

Some night

when you waken to perfect darkness and plush coolness
you might hear the soft thud of wings against a wall
or maybe a windowpane. Large wings, you think. Half in,
half out of sleep. The mind right for an arrival.
Like wingbeats shedding water, though, you know
in the plinth quiet, it's not that.

It gestures an *open door*, as if travel were the only option.

The hallway, newly carpeted in gravel and bent grass.

Afterwards is a hardwood forest, trees spaced with paths.

2

Back of midnight, I see myself off, leave someone
to sleep for me. One field has rain; another none.
A thaw wind, in from the coast, moving up-country.
All sorts of weather are to be expected.
Down a ravine, horses among the myrtle trees
like Zechariah said they'd be. Shrubs, really,
whose sweetness mitigates the smell of death.
My dark siblings, who came this way, further on:
The life ahead of this life, the last bit left to the sleeper.

Reading Montaigne

Every day, he went up the spiral staircase
to the top of his tower, a room of curved shelves,
roof beams covered with writ-out quotations.

Pity the man, he said, *who hasn't a room of his own,*
a room behind the shop. Its entry, a five-foot door
I have to stoop to. Woman, an occasional subject.
Never the audience.
Still, I'm here, wintering over
in the familiarity of his company. *Equilibrium's*
the thing for happiness: Exceptionally good at aloof.
What you'd expect from a tower.
Did I slip there,
make a mis-step on one of the risers? Lose myself
in the stairwell of his spiralling prose?

Pacing the room, he inspected the strangeness
of his own thoughts – or rode them leisurely,
and without plan, to Rome, changing horses en route.

Stored his Catholic faith in a cabinet, went every
whichway with other notions: Provisional as a valise
whose contents could be revised in an addendum.

Travelling, he claimed, has more to do with the mind –
a runaway – than a wickering horse, ground-tied at an inn.

I want a man, he said, *to begin with a conclusion*:
What he never did, or ended there, either. Nor do I.

Stepped out into blustery March to see a warm wind
making nothing of the snow: Unstable as a synopsis.

De Kooning's Door

after *Door to the River*, by Willem de Kooning, 1960

He had no idea how far away from him she could go.

It wasn't that she rebuffed him. She'd been to some ancient place and it had a claim on her.

Of the pictures he might have made in those first weeks, but didn't, one in particular stayed with him – the pair of them sleeping in the sun-shafted bed. Her white shift rucked up, its top buttons undone. The baby on his back in the arc of her body, his arms outflung. His left leg bent at the knee, foot resting on the opposite thigh. The right foot pointing: A dancer's pivot, or an atom's. They were one molecule, her and him.

Had he painted it – in black enamel, maybe, and zinc white – one form would orbit the other.

The planes of her body that he'd known so well. The same way they'd come to know, together, the fields 'round the rented house, the woods fuzzy until you entered, its low-lying leaf beds.

He'd asked her one morning what it felt like, the nursing, and lifting her eyes from the baby, she'd said she could feel it deep down and all through. She sat in the broad-armed chair to nurse, sometimes a book open where the conclusion of the armrest flared wide. An old chair, straight-back, high rush seat. Or she walked the house, pausing at the porchdoor, a downstairs windows, the baby close to her body in its homemade sling.

Soon after its birth, he'd resumed his habit of early-morning drives to the city, to his studio. He was working through what he thought of as his yellow period, the first of those, a portrait of her descending the sloped grainfield. Her arms swishing grainheads. Like a boy playing at airplanes. He'd angled the field the way Degas tilted a shelf in one of his.

Then there was *Pastorale*, but for the longest time now he'd been working on *Door to the River*, with its slabs of upright timbers, a crossbeam between, broad loose strokes of yellow. A barely door. The river a calligraphic blue. He was less of an abstractionist since they'd moved to the country. She was in this one too, wearing her navy coat, mauve from the nearness of the yellow, one stroke, slanted toward the river. Just that.

Wild Honeysuckle

Schooldays, she'd see him off saying,
Don't talk to strangers.

I *am* the stranger, he'd murmur, his satchel bumping
his shoulder blades down the lane. Hedges there,
either side: Cedar overlaid with vines. Honeysuckle.

Down far, the lane curves west. Do you see that –
how quickly she could lose sight of him.

Miry clay in the spring fields.

In the week the trees hung out their leaves –
and we were in the swill of it – he disappeared.

Tentacular tree roots above ground – wet from
the night's rain – had the look of muscles flexing.

She noticed everything – the way you do when worst
worry steps across the verandah, knocks on the door.

He'd gone missing before – a half-day, maybe –
but she'd pulled him home with her heart.
They were like that, wordless and cross-woven.

Sentimental, some'll say, but she knows better than most
the heelstrike of tragedy through the gravel hours. Rackety.

A Mason jar on the window sill warming. Quart-size.
He'd intended to collect frogs' spawn after school.

If he were to come back, the slappy screen door
would be a triumphal arch. His lovely face. The look of him
framed there.

Maybe he'd be wearing the second sight, or the vertical
slit of the eye of the dog. All those years, sweet Jesus,
since she'd naturalized the trumpet creeper, trained it over the hedge.

Son

The aspen grove is one tree. Suckers from shallow roots extend it
over the forest floor.

Interstellar starlings in its mass.

I ask you, What's not joined up?

The wave breaking on the Shediac shore had its start in Galway Bay.

Just so, Your look, your words, go far, go deep, have a source that's
unreachable.

You who are now grown have long since
outdistanced what I know of you.
Tilt of head, turn of phrase, back before me.

Zero

... snow on snow, / in the bleak midwinter, long ago.
Christina Rossetti

The degree at which snow is rain upon impact
so that only the trees – high up – are whitened.
Here below, and indoors, light's disconsolate.

The burlapped hedges making their way to the manger.

Streets away, ever-hopeful children are carolling
snow on snow: Concert moving towards you, same way
a memory – muffled and indistinct – approaches.

You're up the stairs, convinced there's a better view.
Two flights to storage. The tackle of years over the floor.

Where you need to be, dormer at the far end,
'til motion's step-stopped by their thronging –
the unhappy dead under a dim bulb.

They want your company, the way you want the children –
some snow-deep memory in their alto. Choral

lifting off a street corner, intersection where

the accompanist – violin under his arm – steps from the crowd,

whistles you down the stairsteps, gesturing,
all rain is snow above the clouds.

But you can't. The years' mind holds you fast: You're of the end,
not the clear cold breathable beginning.

Truth and Invention

Messengers known and unknown to us moved through the valley.
Some came as peddlers, carrying notions – needles, zippers, snaps.

Naturally enough, the women welcomed them. One or two
were tailors. Their leather satchels opened a glint of contents.

The stories they told turned the rough texture of work
to smooth fable. We could see they were sizing us up.

Others were salt merchants following the river inland.
Theirs were the oldest stories, old as rock deposits:

It's not frost brines the rooves, they said. The dead leaving,
leave a trace.

We knew better – knew meat, milk, and lard's
nothing more than meat, milk, lard.

Showed them seasonal signs – raptors riding thermals south,

goats abandoning the steep flanks of the valley, a cohort
of clouds leaning on the lid of West Mountain.

By mid-December, frost quakes echoed side to side.

The slope-shouldered men believed the quarter moon an omen,
claimed the mildness of St. Stephen's was snow reversing
into the sky shed.

It's true, days have peaks and troughs. Why wouldn't they?

In the valley, everything's an image of the mountain,
no man can make that up.

Dear ____________,

It was a book that made me long for men so far away.

Claire-Louise Bennett, *Pond*

If you want, come early winter. I'll be airing out the quilts and will make up a bed for you. The winter is downy all through. The house turns its back on windows and looks inward. Don't forget to bring the hooded cloak Sebastian gave you – a useful blanket on cold nights. The south-going geese follow the riverway but, from the train, you can come by fields. Just now, there's a skiff of snow on the ground, a slick on the long pond in the horse pasture.

For six, seven weeks, the house is January dusk at all hours 'til one evening you're coming down the stairs to start supper and you see the south windows ablaze. And that very day, the first day of March, the first day of Lent, you see that all the plants – the plants you'd brought indoors – have tipped their leaves to the pane. Window and windowsill – the plant-lined sill – will have turned their attention to the solemn assembly of crows working the season from spongy earth, and you too, pilgrim, will have turned.

Onrush

Present-tense, mild with moisture.

Ground that was white, bronzed by overnight rain.
Rocks and boulders sweated and shiny. *Ah ha, the spring.*

Out into, I say. Past the deer – same colour as ground – nosing a garden bed for new growth.
Be off, spindly shanks. Away with you.

Past the horse chestnut, buds wound tight – hinges heat will open to hallucinatory colour.
And further,

The river, in its freshet, rising – raising a brown tantrum. Juicy muck at the brink of it
and next-to-no foothold. *And yes*, to its rush and to the air's uplift
and to the feather-plucking crows in pairs, courting not quarrelling.

And that *churring* sound. Night-migrating sparrows here now, and everywhere these firsts.

The uppity air hasn't breath for bygones.

The Extra

Because he's quiet as the tomb, I babble into the still and poignant air.

Always about, he rarely shows himself, so don't be expecting to see him.

One time in the garden – this was last spring – when I was knelt to the raised bed
deadheading the fritillaria, also known as Imperial Crown, he was behind me,
spading a drainage ditch, the lowliest job. The aroma of cedar root rising.

It's easy to be mistaken about the gardener.

The coverall is, of course, a disguise.

2

He's the cicerone of heaven. Should you go there, he'll show you round the
antiquities.
The tree of knowledge in gold leaf. Its fruit, jewelled baubles. Purely decorative.

The tree of life, much as it was millennia ago, its rough bark fragrant to the touch.
Cypress or cedar – a complex scent no one's ever been able to decipher.

In your lifetime, you'll have known trees like that, upright in the house built around it,
the girth of it bulking in every storey, crown over the rooftop.

Three Waltzes That Haven't Names

In the foyer of an asylum, a curving staircase, wrought-iron. No chairs or benches. Halfway up the stairs, there's a man in a grey suit. Dignified. Left hand on the railing. Where his eyes should be, there are pieces of granite. I go up to him. Touch his sleeve. He tells me about a winter so cold stones froze. He was saying mass, two masses: One for the congregation, one for himself, something about what he'd done. It was at that point in the mass when he'd come down the chancel to read the gospel. The Blessed Virgin in the nave, cracked from the cold, toppled over. The fragments blinded him. Did he say this? Did he explain his eyes? I took him by the arm, led him to an upper room. Begin again, I said.

In the foyer of an asylum, he said, where the light's astonishing, there was a woman midway on the stairs.

2

Pre-dawn, a man in a dark overcoat leaves a hotel by cab. In the darkness of the backseat, he says to no one, to himself, "You don't know vulnerability until you've been a passenger." He has the cabbie pull up in front of the airport, watches people pour out the exits on their way to parking or the taxistand or shuttle. Sometimes that's enough. Other times, he dismisses the cab and goes inside, stands beneath the Arrivals sign, watching people come down the escalator. He hopes to see a couple, a man and wife.

They always took the overnight. Business class. At first, she minded sleeping in public, but got used to it, learned, like him, to love the cocooning – the cabin's dimmed lights, the low hum of others' conversation, warmed blankets.

On the escalator, the wife is a step behind her husband, her hand on his shoulder. She's carrying a camel coat over one arm, and a book-heavy backpack which makes her look childlike. At the bottom, there's the usual shuffling on the last step, the firmness of the floor, a surprise.

The man in the dark overcoat leaves the airport, takes a cab to the office. It's how he begins each day when he's in this city. The airport, the watching.

3

The grey-suited man's in a café. On his own, as it happens. A century before, its pale blue walls and high windows must have been someone's frontroom. Angel cornice in plaster, gone ivory. Odd for a café, high and airy. Mid-afternoon's the best time for light and emptiness. Just that one person – a woman at a corner table, dipping biscotti in a coffee bowl, bent elbow holding her book open. Intentness. She's got on a fawn felt cloche. Below it, her hair bunches out. He hasn't a book or newspaper. Never has. Fingertips tapping the table edge, there's inward listening in his expression. He's as close to sleep, while waking, as it's possible to be.

When she rises to go, nodding to the server, the blind man senses she's taller, more attractive, than he'd thought. She shoves a colloquial hand through her hair, loosening what the hat had pressed down.

Coming in, the man in the overcoat holds the door for her. A look – recognition or apology – passes between them. There's indecision in the way he scrunches his gloves in one hand. Like a man deciding direction in a train station. You might suppose he's there for the stoneblind but, no, it's the reader he wants. Sometimes, one fiction crosses over into another.

Vernal Wedding

Dusk, and the men are drinking beer by the tailgate of Benny's Ford,
their jackets slung over the truckbox, sleeves rolled up. The huddle of them.

Their up-and-down voices reach me in the ballroom. My lime-green sheath
holds me hostage during Mrs. Crane's organza approval of the bride.

The groom slow-waltzing in the arms of his wife wants to be with them too.

Rural men move in herds. They are vivid and seasonal.

On the job, they swerve-shift the way birds do, one brain
moving over a field: Seedlings precision-planted in drills –
a vernacular perfection by evening. Field of forethought,

not that anyone, apart from the almanac, planned it.
They're connected in ways the bride brigade's not.

Blame it on my brothers, an upbringing in their image –
for me they wanted the cardinal's flame red, not the mate's dull green.

Rain, Versailles

after the photograph *The Private Apartment of Madame du Barry at Versailles*,
by Deborah Turbeville, 1981

Everything built has a rain shadow – an area where rain can't reach.
The court gardeners never plant close to the palace. No moisture.

They're experts on the physics of falling rain, its exact slant
relative to wind swerve. Know the likelihood descent's lateral.

Odd how we think otherwise. Feel it falling on the body, blunt
from above, the way ground drinks rain – indifferent to direction.

In the rain shadow we're most likely to see it as vertical:
The scrim of it a drop-down opacity convincing us – me and Maria.

Other delusions: A straight back and scarce speech secures approval.

While we pace the shadow's dry corridor, the barberry hedge –
a good two feet from the wall – grows glossy in the downpour.

Rain days, we march our leisure between hedge and house.
Our patent leather slippers in the scree, hems on the ground.

I've been thinking of the back-room furniture dressed in dust covers.
The little rooms where we waited to be chosen.

Apparitional women, non-existent unless summoned,
moving slick as indoor rain over the parquet flooring.

And then we weren't – chosen, I mean. The shadow walk's not so bad
'though I can't be convinced a downfall changes course.

With Tomas and Bertie at the Sallyforth Café

Tomas, who claims there's a ceremony for everything, carefully
pours milky coffee into a china bowl, sops buttered bread in the last bit.
Habits originating in a house he's not lived in for some sixty years.
Back then, he'd prop a book against a cream pitcher and read.

Off with the horses,
his parents complained, but these days he's the impresario
of our gatherings, eager for talk. What we're all doing here.

As the horse hopes for the halter, we wait for what lurks.

What's worse, Bertie asks, *diminishment or death*?
She hates to think of mind and memory emptied of contents.
And haven't we still the bodies of racehorses?

The one who sits into the saddle and draws us up behind
knows what he's about, knows, sooner or later, we'll slip
our arms around his waist. Go willingly. After days or weeks
dawdling about at the edge of the woods, we'll enter forest.

They say a dreamer never arrives at his destination.
Perhaps the same is true of death – endless travel.

Tomas, who's all about arrivals, and the ceremony
appropriate to them, is having none of it. He folds
his napkin, straightens his bowtie (red paisley), as if
the clatter of hooves were already rattling the teacups.

Lear Prunes the Black Currant Bush

The *Arborists' Guide* advises secateurs for a clean, angled cut. As directed, Lear chooses the oldest wood – moss-thickened branches – follows each branch to the base and clips. Sap surfaces. When he carries the first armload to the bin, its juices seep into his jacket. *For vigorous new growth*, the *Guide* says, *prune the old.* He resists making an analogy, moves on to the rose bush and the lilac. He's sixty-five, fixes his own supper at night, reads *Tamburlaine* for the unendingness of it. The ground is littered now with the gnarled and the thorny, far more than will fit in the bin. Burning's best, he thinks, something ceremonial on the headland. Since there isn't a promontory in sight, he settles for the camomile sod-bench he built for the girls summers ago, shrunken now, but still possessing some elevation. He wanders into the birch wood, gathers bits of bark, dry twigs. The lopped-off sizzles in a pitch of heat. Overhead, the geese wedge the sky, the satirical sparkle of the river runs on. The season, stooping towards solstice, clutches its twice-night of bedimmed days.

Sex and Death at the Natural History Museum

The once-beautiful meet Wednesdays at the Sallyforth Café.
Late afternoon when light lessens. Easy on the skin. Complimentary.
Bertie, fresh from her nap, says four o'clock is the best of hours.

The men, in their wiry vigour, handle the chairs.
Their hands nicely manicured – cuticles pushed back – the women pour.

The smell of their face powder might remind you of a closed room in warm weather.

A summer wind tilts the empty rockers on the patio.
Forward and backward, their talk.

There are no impostors at the Formica tables. They're beyond that.
They know what they are, and were. A profile never changes.

Touching her wrist, Angus says, *'though bones thin out, they still define.*

Widows and widowers, their mates have preceded them into the coal-sack dark.

Theirs is the speech of those speaking the unutterable.
Also, stories from the past in dignified repose.

When we girls were twelve, Bertie says, *our plaited braids were scissored off.*
Our childhood shorn, we were sent to the dressmaker. A seamstress
married to a taxidermist. They worked opposite ends of the living's lifestory.

Mrs. Salter, I remember, pronounced her husband an immortalist,
denying the decay of beauties in their furred or feathered coats.

Bertie pauses a moment, thinking about the red voile made to match her ribboned shoes.

The button eyes of the fox had their eye on me. Glass-fronted cases
and overhead, owls – both large and small – suspended on wires down

the low-lit hallway. The sewing room, its conclusion or commencement,
depending on your view. Boston ferns cascading from plant stands.

Angus waves his hands about, indicating the overhead. A memory's occurred to him:
Beached whales were trucked to the bug barn. Brought here after, whistle-clean.

In the museum's west gallery, a short walk from the café, there's a suspension of
skeletons,
enormous things you walk beneath. Bones yellowing over time.

Bertie, who danced a quadrille in those ribboned shoes, says
You might want to know about the Greenland shark who lives for centuries.
Sex at a hundred. Winks into silence.

The Mind at sixes and sevens

The Brain is – Wider than the Sky –

Emily Dickinson

Now that all's contracted to an acre, inch-by-inch familiar,
I've taken to talking to Emily. *It was the same for me*, she says,
and it's nothing to complain about since The Outer –
from the Inner / Derives its Magnitude –

I confess a yearning for nighttime train travel,
abstract landscapes in plate glass windows;
a hotel room, arrived at past midnight,
the lamps on low, and the city decorating the dark
with pinprick glitter. Where I can be away in a book,
its paragraphs mimicking the train's momentum
'til overleaf proves otherwise: A word pivoting a room
and I'm back to where I came from.

Unlike mine, her sense of velocity, starting from the regular, is scaled to sky.

The raptor mind, she tells me, seizes its quarry in the least smallholding.

How Memory Works

The frost heaves the past above ground – spoon, coin, stone blade.
Deep down things you'll not find by digging. Just so, there are memories
you couldn't reach even if you wanted to.

And then someone tosses you a phrase – small as a coin – and you're years gone.
Another epoch unfolding in your mind all because Aggie said *bread sandwiches*.

> A woman bringing a field-tea to the men at harvest time.
> Sandwiches wrapped in a damp cloth to keep them fresh –
> *bread sandwiches* – and tea in mason jars, the jars in wool sleeves.
> Tea the colour of a sedimentary river in spring time. The cups
> they're pouring it into are discards – railway dishware, creamy-white and heavy.
> Unbreakable. (The cup's weight, the thick lip of it.) Yes, but what else?
> They're sitting in the shade of the threshing machine. Chaff wandering the air.
> One of them is eating apple cuts from the tip of a pocket knife.
> That'd be Uncle Ollie.
> The thronged past you didn't know
> until you were tipped off. All back. All back then.

Unfinished

It wasn't a grand house, really, but one of its rooms, maybe because of its history, insinuated itself into my future. The entire house was built around a room that had started out as a shop – a workshop where an aeronautical engineer, widowed early on, invented the variable-pitch propeller.

By the time I came to know it, the room, rectilinear and high-ceilinged, was hung, east to west, with a half-dozen translucent curtains, the length of them left loose to flap in the breeze entering by way of the propped-open industrial doors. The gusty air swept the fabric up and over, and around, the grouped armchairs that seemed, even when empty, to lean toward one another. I should mention the mirrors, positioned on the west wall to reflect, no doubt, the swoop of the curtains. When they were tied back, as they were sometimes, the swag of them, toppling over their ropes, obscured the tin ceiling, stencilled with a chart of the stars. In one of the curtained areas an adjustable draughting stool was positioned near the head of a day-bed.

The meridian
lounge-chair, as it was called in those days, was intended for rest at mid-day. But whose rest? And why didn't I ever see anyone there on my clandestine visits? With the rest of the house locked up, and unfinished, who wouldn't – steel doors open in all weathers – gape at the length and height and motion of that room, its overhead of storm-driven clouds.

Years later, when I became the occupant of a similar couch – a place of unrest – that doctor who was famous for his understanding of interiors, showed me into the locked house, introduced me to the woman in possession of my mind. In whatever's shut away, he said, there's always one object that's a cipher for what you know but shouldn't know.

Trees, Yuletide

It was more than melancholy afflicting the clever branch of that family.
This sadness, the risible one said to her therapist, *Is this what consciousness is,*
and is it the same for everyone?

For comics and poets, yes, but not for scholars. They have their archives.
Oddly enough, scientists, raking their facts, are also free of it.

At home it's as innocuous as air, an idler asleep in a chair, but when I'm out and about,
it trails behind, exhales its somatic breath over my left shoulder.

My sadness, she said to the pharmacist, nodding leftward. She had impeccable manners.

Is it lack of sleep, she asked the doctor – physician to the family for decades.
He was slumped in his swivel, condoling their names. She touched the nearness
of his elbow, felt the tweed's saturation.

In reception, a half dozen patients: Outside, near the plate glass window,
a crowd of shapes fogging the view, their foreheads leant on the patients' reflection.

Not far from home, she pulled onto the shoulder, walked the path to the river. The trees, undecorated, were shadows of their former selves.

December is the worst, she said to no one, to the trees. *Impersonation never holds up.*
Sooner or later the limbs give out.

Sun After

Otherwise, a white plain; the house adrift squints at loneliness.
Snow smuts on the windowpane,
                                        and in the stormporch,
the tools of another season are collared in snow.

There's sunshine after blizzard, but you can't remember
what that means for roots. Bulbs, beyond recall.

The hibernal mind hasn't more than a month's reach. All roads
to the interior, skittish.

The respite from winter, midwinter, is a state for which
there's no name.

Stand the doors open. Let the house sample the leeward.

The infirm, quilted in long nights, will succumb in spring.
Wearing dark coats, the removal men will raven them away.

On the summit of the stairs, you hear your dead father say,
It'll be a large day when things milden up.

The rarity of white birds

All through the house we took down the winter draperies. Put up the summer.
Sheers, they're called. Pale as albino sparrows. Flights of near-nothing
we tied back at evening. Eager for the cooler air squaring up to windows.

We never learned the solstitial ease of habit others have.

Not like the trees: Weeks back, they hung out their glossy miscellany
in rain-saturated air – bundles unfolding in sage, celadon, yellowcake,
before ripening to emerald,

an overall lightweight cladding that shamed our lag-time.

Or the snow geese, high up, travelling narrow corridors north.
Half the year spent in to-and-fro migration. Their white plumage
suiting the clouds. Polar arrival perfectly timed.

The Shotgun in Gainsborough's Landscape

after *Robert Andrews and His Wife*, by Thomas Gainsborough, c. 1748-50

How short a time, she said, giving my father her hand. She kept her eyes on his face, scanning it, as if the last sentence might be found there. We watched her watching him. Her four-word fragment rose on the last syllable, sighed off. A relative of some degree, she'd come to stay. Uncle Ollie brought her, which wasn't unusual: We were the ones to billet invalid relations recovering from this or that. My mother, who was Charlotte's opposite in every way, would find her a place, as she had the others, the ones with rheumatic fever or a tubercular look. She'd prepare an upstairs bed and see to it that us kids took turns bringing Charlotte a tray at mealtime. Although she was whippet-thin, Charlotte's convalescence wouldn't be entirely bedridden: She hadn't the cough of the tubercular or the rosy colouring of the rheumatic. Still, there was something amiss about her.

I didn't know if she was a child or an adult. Maybe somewhere between. She was wearing a sea-blue dress, silk I'd guess, and had the smallest feet, shod in what my mother would say were not sensible shoes. Like the small-footed woman in the Gainsborough print in the parlour: An invalidish bride beside her upright gun-and-dog husband, his shot-ready gaze fixed on the prospect. Charlotte might have had a gentry shoe-size, but she hadn't the accoutrements – gun, dog, and husband. Valuable I'd say, in that order.

My mother was tall and bony and always in motion. Her sentences (complete) tended to direction or instruction – *Fetch in the wash* or *Bring a bottle of plum from the jam cupboard*. She kept her conversation for the evening and for my father, a murmur deep-down in our sleep. He was a great believer in the benefits of fresh air so windows were lifted to the limit and kept that way the whole summer. During the heat spell that brought us Charlotte, the nighttime thunder stuttered like fireworks and brought no rain. Neither did the dusty daytime winds, which are nowhere to be seen in the Gainsborough. Some landscapes have no weather. *The noise of it in the trees*, as Charlotte might say, wiping gunstock oil on her blue dress.

Talk Puts an End to Time

There's no one left to impress. The hall's empty, audience gone.

Raked seats stare at the podium.

In the boardroom, the chairs are tilted against the table as if the cleaner's been
through.
October light picks up the sheen of the tabletop. Tosses it in the bin.

Down every avenue, hedgerows obscure housefronts.

Warehouses on the waterfront have been empty half a century.

2

Soon as you step out pronominally, the risk of losing arises:
What a spendthrift, the first-person. Shouldn't it be more watchful?
And careful? Nothing, nobody, by way of support: Atlas-shouldered,
it insists on vertical opinions 'til, sooner or later, it's addressing bare walls.

3

In the barnloft of a deserted farm we stood in the light angling through split boards.
This was years back. The thing is, the loft was full of clover as if cattle – restless
below –
were waiting for their nightfeed. Warm and breathy in their stanchions. Presence
can be that near. The thoroughbred, fidgety in its boxstall, rippling the emptiness.

4

Until yesterday, I'd forgotten how time works its way through,
how it might illumine house windows, pedestrians on the street, ships at anchor.

On a day of steady rain, how to summon it back, be of it?

In the small hours

In the small hours, a single vehicle on a wet street washes
other lives into sleep. Someone out drinking his grief.

Nighttime mind on the prowl, down alleyways. Bin-feeder
going through the rubbish. Noodling.

In night's single-digit district, he can be whoever he wants –
nightwalker, panhandler, go-preacher. Or, the man in the half-ton,

a quart of Bacardi in the glove compartment.
(How lightly he wears his name. A daytime accessory.)

The woman who taps on the passenger window
mouths something ruby-red that could be a number.

Later, when light's grit-grey, squat fog sits in an upholstered chair.
What slid through the screen is pocked. Some of it climbs the
    stairs.

Uses of: Fog's a substance that can mature a memory

or cure stains from linens if hung on the line. Did he read that
somewhere or invent it? The mind's a pick-up. Both senses.

Swimmers

Our self ... fish-like inhabits deep seas and plies obscurities
threading her way between the boles of giant weeds ....
Virginia Woolf, *Mrs. Dalloway*

Knowing the day will brighten, they hang laundry in fog.
Wearing old coats, my mother and my sister, disappear into the blur.
It's March and still cold. A slow snow-melt. Winter's moult.

Damp clothes to damp air: I'm the baffled youngest behind glass.

From time to time, one arm, and then another, lifts –
swimmers stroking through water. I'd seen the same
when my brothers swam the river, arms lifting spray.

Afterwards, they told me about the grasses on the riverbed,
an underwater meadow only a swimmer gets to see – what
can't be brought to the surface.

Lengths of fabric, whiter than mist, appear at the far end of the line.
As if mother and daughter were patching relationship onto nothingness.
The semaphore of sheets show they're moving, unseen, back toward me.

Even so, I don't really know who they are, who I am. And even now.

Memory's not an enfilade, doors perfectly aligned, so you can see
to the start. It's a window, watery glass distorting all the way back.

Window

There's always been two of us and I'm not talking siblings. As for them, we were an even dozen if you count the one after me who didn't make it, that boy who would have been beloved, being last, being broken, something like a wing where his left arm should have been, those who fashioned him reluctant to let him go *or* stay, and the sweetest voice ever, no speech but it was song. Not that he'd had the chance, but it's what was said after, or so I've heard. Barely beyond infancy, what did I know? An either-day boy, born on the midnight hour of the fall equinox, one of those times when the door swings open and whatever crosses over. In the after-telling, *the year's four ways*, was their way of explaining the boy.

A window not unlike other pastoral windows – four rectangular panes making up the whole – although smaller than the others, narrower and nearer to the floor. Like those Lilliputian doors leading to out-of-the-way places – cellars and summer pantries – a window looking out on the garden, its long stretch of lawn, and beyond that, the woods. A man – was it a man, though – in a high-collared greatcoat, caped and flaring, standing at the bottom of the garden where the woods began, the tops of the trees misted – it was back of midnight or it was early morning – the trunks themselves dark from the damp but clear of the mist. Coming out of the woods or about to enter, but for now motionless, his attention fixed on the irregular window.

If there was to be a homebirth – and they were all that – the younger ones were to be sent away, but why bestir them from their beds when they were sleeping soundly?

A window suited to size, its crosspiece grubby with impatience. Mine.

That's the thing about siblings. I could have been any of the sleepers that night, could have been the oldest attending with the aunts, or the brother who'd hurried away for the doctor or, even, the boy with the twisted arm.

Then, or during the rainfall days that followed, shifts of that sort ended, other ways opened.

A yellowish fox, a cross-shaped patch on its shoulders, nosing the long grass. The man who'd set him down there turning back for the woods. The supple-limbed trees reaching down to him. What I learned later, the cross fox, named for its markings, is the most domestic of creatures, its shyness, whether natural or augmented by angels, letting you be exactly who you are. Ferocity 'round you like a coat.

Evening, a resistance

The old storytellers who said *time will fail if I tell all*
knew the math of words-times-hours, but what of the opposite:
Words that can't deliver the hour? Here in the valley,
with a river through it, evening refuses to write its story:
The tall trees – wreathed 'round with something smoky –
surveil a hushed decorum. A smokiness that thins out
just below imperious crowns. How not to harm
the green-washed-with-grey quiet of it all?
Time, I should have known, is on the side of the trees.
Skirting our every effort to know them.

Root

Late August, and the die-down's begun. Alert-green leaves
are crisped at their edges, the grass a burnt umber.
Roots spiralling downward make notes on summer growth –
the effect of parch on the size and duration of blooms.
Already, the seedpods – bronzed and bullet-hard – are bent
to another season. Their tips leant westward. We take our cue
from them. Anything done now is about next year. Something
in us subsides, while the prudent part of the brain feels its way deeper.

Are leaf and bloom the expression of root, and is that trifecta
repeated in us? Do we prize the showy parts when, all along,
it's the buried bit deserves the credit? Nothing attractive about it:
No one carts a ganglia of roots to the flower stall. Or admits
the higher mind – its sonatas and songs – owes a deep-down debt.

Come spring, there'll be the tiniest cursive on the leaves of plants,
blooms will exhale a fragrance that's three-fold sweeter in lower ground.

Letter

Yours, of some years back, is on the dresser. The sending of it smudged – date, month, and year. Sometimes late at night, the sentences of my reply form so perfectly, paragraphs unfold beginning to end. But in the morning all's fled. Fledden. Flod.

This is how it happens: On the first cool day of fall, you put on a warm coat, find a scarf, and go out. Somewhere in the hedge maze, you get to thinking about the books you've read, the affiliations among them, plot gone to plot. Soon enough,

the spring melt is making gutters in the garden. A steady drip from the downspout, and around the base of the elm, the sprout of something. The tawny ground was there all along.

At our age, a swathe of time can feel like a day: How like to gods we are in these ratios.

I knew a painter once – this was in Gascony – who whitened paper with paint and put it away for six or seven years 'til it ivoried over. Then painted the thing he'd been thinking about all those years back. The interval, you see, counts for nothing. I have your last – yours of yesterday – right handy. It was yesterday, wasn't it?

Tree

for JWS

My sparrow, my sweetheart, thou are so seeming small, having here, at thy sickbed, arrived.

Anon. 14th century

That maple in my neighbour's yard is, for me, the epitome of tree.
Mornings in early spring, its arrangement of buds is a small electric works,
and in summer, O in summer, it flings its head about, flounces its greenery.
The tree triumphant.

Such symmetry in its high-up branching:
All around, its outer limbs curve inward, cupping the crown, lifting it.
Alone on its patch of ground, it owns, even when bare, a regal indifference.
Trees by Colville have the same look.

Now, though, the season's turned.
A wind from the north, rumour in its veins, has swung overland.
Sure there'll be apple days – sun on the windfall – but something's concluding.
Endings, who can bear them?

As you say, in this country leaves redden east to west.
A week or so, and I'll be living with a flagrancy of colour.
What's that about? Grief so vascular, it bleeds through?

You'll see how I've tried to write the poem of the tree and how all along
it was you. Not even on my own property. You never were, and yet, from every angle,
you filled the windows wherever I looked.

Notes

"Supper, *The Iliad*" follows Richard Lattimore's translation of *The Iliad,* but deviates here and there from his account.

In "Tablecloth and Other Compound Words," the italicized line is from *Tatler* #205, quoted in the *OED.*

In "The Supper-painter considers *The Symposium,*" a two-word phrase is quoted from Walter Hamilton's translation of *The Symposium.*

"Patterns, Palm Sunday": *Our epiphanies inseparable from our chores* appears in "Virginia Woolf: The Emergent Self," an essay in Jonah Lehrer's *Proust Was Neuroscientist.* The italicized part of the fourth line comes from the essay "Mark Strand on Edward Hopper," *The New York Review of Books* 25 June 2015: 40-41. In *Woman / Image / Text*, Lynne Pearce grieves the fact that "women come with their rooms attached."

"Sleeping in the Spare" quotes 2 Corinthians 12:3.

"*Dream* as Misnomer": In *The Other Night: Dreaming, Writing, and Restlessness in Twentieth-Century Literature*, Herschel Farbman uses the phrase "what wakes when we sleep" to an entirely different purpose.

"Morning, convex mirror": Jan van Eyck spelled his name in that way when he wrote *Johannes de Eyck fuit hic* on the *Arnolfini* painting.

"Reading Montaigne" reflects upon, and quotes, *The Complete Essays of Montaigne*, trans. Donald M. Frame, which I read in tandem with Sarah Bakewell's *How to Live or A Life of Montaigne in one question and twenty attempts at an answer.*

"Zero": The "year's mind" is a Roman Catholic requiem mass held on the anniversary of a person's death. I've used the term in the plural.

"Son" is for Quentin Compton Papenhausen, and for his son, Robbie.

In "Rain, Versailles," the epigraph refers to *The Private Apartment of Madame du Barry at Versailles*, by Deborah Turbeville, which appears in her book of photographs *Unseen Versailles.*

"*The Brain – is Wider than the Sky –*": In addition to the Emily Dickinson line quoted in the title, the poem quotes "The Outer – from the Inner / Derives its Magnitude" from Dickinson.

Acknowledgements

My thanks to the editors who published some of these pieces in their journals:

Encore Magazine: "Onion"

Malahat Review: "Tablecloth and Other Compound Words," "Sleeping in the Spare," and "The River in Spring"

The Fiddlehead: "Some Night," "Wild Honeysuckle," and "Truth and Invention"

"Wifecakes" appeared, under a different title and in a slightly different version, in *Singular*, the catalogue for the exhibition of that title by visual artist Suzanne Hill. New Brunswick Museum Exhibition Centre, Saint John, NB. November 2016.

To my son Aaron, always my first reader, my love and thanks.

To my ever-wonderful and forthright editor, Evan Jones, thank-you for your guidance.

My thanks to Richard Dionne for the many ways in which he helped.

Aboout Anne Compton

A two-time winner of the Atlantic Poetry Prize, Anne Compton won the Governor General's Award for Poetry for *Processional*, her second collection; and the Raymond Souster Award for *Alongside*, her fourth. Finding a place on numerous shortlists, Compton's work appears in *The Best of the Best Canadian Poetry*. In 2008, she was awarded the Alden Nowlan Award for Excellence in English Language Literary Arts and the Lieutenant-Governor's Award for High Achievement in English Language Literary Arts in 2014. A former teacher and writer-in-residence at the University of New Brunswick at Saint John, her most recent prose book, *Afterwork: Essays on Literature and Beauty*, appeared in 2017.